New Tracks

Demystifying
the Art
of
Writing Good

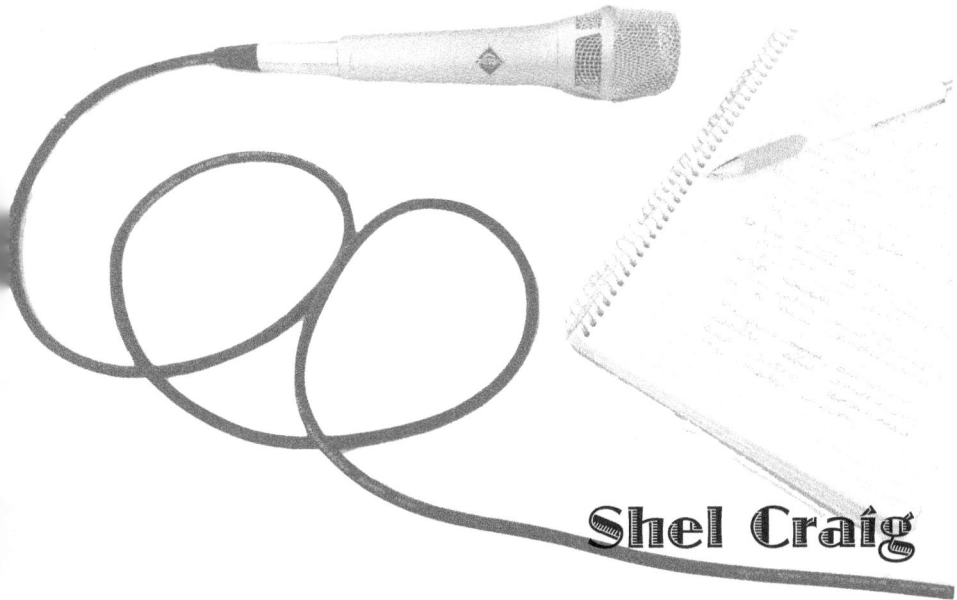

Shel Craig

For Chris

Contents

Introduction

Lyric writing really isn't as difficult as you might imagine it to be. After hearing your favorite artists describe how they came up with their best songs, it may seem extraordinary, but they've had years of practice and many attempts that didn't work. Most of them started out just as awkwardly as you, then learned, practiced, and improved.

Many would-be lyricists are so intimidated by the prospect of writing lyrics that they never begin. They believe there is a secret recipe that only the talented know. Others make the entire process more difficult for themselves by agonizing over a single word or phrase for days, weeks, or even months. There is no secret and no sense aiming for perfection; it'll keep you stranded. The best way to become good is to simply begin. You'll learn as you go.

Writing lyrics is a process that should be neither too hard, nor too easy. It'll take patience and practice. In the beginning, you'll likely want to dash off the first thing that comes to mind and be done with it. This isn't a bad place to start, but if you want to improve the quality of those initial attempts, you'll want to put in some effort.

I'll tell you a secret: not everything you write is going to be great. Let that be okay. The process of writing is what is important. For every lyric you feel good about, there will be many, many more that will only seem passable or won't quite feel right. This is good. It means you aren't settling, and it means you have a will to improve. As with anything else, the more you practice, the better you'll get.

One trap you might find yourself falling into is comparing your lyrics to those of others. Be cautious about this. Study the lyrics of those you admire, but don't expect the same level of quality. It may also be tempting to compare your lyrics to those of your friends or other local musicians, but this isn't helpful either. Theirs are not right and yours wrong, or vice versa. Every person has a unique perspective and unique experiences. Focus on your own improvement, and you'll begin to feel good enough about your work that you won't resort to comparisons.

If you enjoy wordplay or storytelling, you'll find lyric writing enjoyable, too; however, if the idea of crafting lyrics sounds like a dull chore, you may need to awaken your interest. Those of you who enjoy listening, thinking about, or discussing the lyrics in songs may find you enjoy writing lyrics more than you'd imagined. Don't think of it as a task on your to-do list but as an opportunity to be creative and to express yourself in a new way.

It is my hope that you find this book helpful in getting started on your own path to lyric writing and that you learn to enjoy not just the end product but the process itself.

When you're having fun, ideas will begin to flow. Okay, let's begin!

Chapter 1

Finding Ideas

Ideas can come from many sources: dreams, snippets of conversation, a funny turn of a phrase, or just about anywhere. Writing hit songs is not my area of expertise, so I will not be delving into that. There are plenty of resources available should you want to look into that further, but my goal is to get you started.

My ideas tend to start with an interesting phrase or topic, but sometimes I follow my mind and let it bring up connections I wouldn't consciously make. I use timed writing exercises to elicit connections, ideas, and even lyric lines.

Timed Writing

For timed writing, I use a plain notebook and pen and the timer on my phone. You can use a kitchen timer, stopwatch, or any other gadget that can alert you when you've reached 10 minutes or more. You can use a computer for this exercise as well, but if you don't type particularly fast, I suggest good, old fashioned cursive writing.

Open your notebook to a new page. At the top, write the name of your topic. Pick any topic— a memory, an event, a plate on the kitchen table, last night's dishes

—it really doesn't matter what. Don't get hung up on finding the perfect topic. The purpose of the exercise is to get you into descriptive thinking.

Next, set your timer for 10 minutes and start it. Write without stopping or pausing for the full 10 minutes. Write anything that pops into your head as quickly as you can. Don't go for rhyme or rhythm now. Just write. Be descriptive. What does it look like? Do you hear anything? Are you touching something, and, if so, how does that feel?

Note: It's important not to censor what you're writing or correct your spelling at this time.

Go with whatever comes to mind, no matter how uncomfortable that might seem. There is weight, emotion, and interesting stuff in discomfort.

Read through your timed writing. Circle any lines or ideas that seem particularly interesting.

In future timed writings, try to get beyond simple descriptions. How else could you describe it? What does it remind you of? Could you relate it to something else?

Example: Sweeter than Macintosh, softer too. Like biting into crispy dessert. The skin as radiant as a newly washed fire engine.

Don't worry about whether it makes sense or not. Just follow your mind wherever it goes. That apple might take you to the field you played in, the red bike you got for your birthday, or the first time you hit a baseball. Let it. This is how you find the really good stuff.

Our minds are cagey, so don't toss your old writing notebooks thinking there's nothing in them worth salvaging. You'd be surprised by the gems you've missed. When I'm having a bit of a dry spell, I revisit some of my old timed writings. I read through several, looking for things that didn't stand out before. Usually it's been months since I wrote them, and I'm often surprised to find nearly complete ideas, structure, phrasing, or at least the start of something.

Not all writing will be full of buried gems, though. Sometimes, there is something you needed to write out of your system. That's okay, too, as long as it's not the only writing you do. Explore feelings, imagery, stories, events— all of it.

When to Write

This is the part where you have to know yourself, at least a bit. I am not someone who likes schedules much. I have a general time of day when I prefer to write, but I'm not rigid about it. I do write every weekday, however. If you're someone who likes schedules or is likely to bypass writing if it's left unscheduled, I suggest you set a time of day or at least pop a reminder in your calendar. Many writers advocate morning writing because this is when our internal critic is likely to be a little fuzzy. This hasn't worked well for me, but I suggest you give it a try. It might be when you get your best ideas. My point is, experiment with what works for you. You don't want to feel rushed, so getting up early to write before work may not be the best plan. It's up to you.

Right about now you might be saying, "But I don't want to write novels, I want to write lyrics!" It all comes from the same place. I guarantee that if you do these timed writing sessions, your ideas will be much more vivid than simply trying to string lines together cold. After a time, you'll find that interesting phrases will pop into your head and string themselves together all on their own, but don't wait for these. They are your rewards for having put in the work.

To really rev up your pool of ideas, I suggest you read one of Natalie Goldberg's writing books. Writing Down the Bones is the best known, but any of them are a good place to start.

There are plenty of exercises in each to get you thinking and writing on a daily basis.

On to the next part . . .

Finding Interesting Lines

So what constitutes an interesting line or idea? Any phrase that seems interesting to you— that feels like it could have more to offer or a story to tell—is a line worth investigating.

You'll need to use instinct, and as you practice, your instinctual choices will become better. It should be fairly obvious that a line such as 'I'm looking in the window' doesn't elicit much emotion, but a line such as 'I'm on the outs but looking in' prompts more questions. Why doesn't this person go inside? What makes him/her an outsider? Look for lines that prompt you to ask questions or wonder.

About those Circled Lines

I have a few pages at the back of my writing notebook where I keep a list of phrases I've encountered in my timed writing, or elsewhere, that piqued my curiosity. I write my circled lines there. When I have another line or two to add, I write those down in the back as well. If I feel like I might have at least the start of a lyric, though, I write the lines on a new page in my notebook and begin work. We'll look at this a bit more in the next section.

You may choose to keep a separate notebook or file for your circled lines and interesting ideas. Your goal should be to make these lines/ideas as accessible as possible. Use whatever method works best for you. You'll find these lines valuable when you're looking for a new jumping-off point for timed writing or when you want to start writing a lyric.

Turning Circled Lines into Lyric Lines

This is where the work begins.

The best way to start is to consult your list of circled lines/ideas, and choose one that stands out to you. Don't just pick the first one on the list. Pick one that has feeling attached, sparks a memory, or creates a picture in your mind when you read it. These have weight and, therefore, have somewhere for the idea to travel. Sometimes you'll find that another line or two will immediately jump to mind when you read your circled line. Begin there.

Write your selected line on a new page. Write any other lines you think of beneath it. Keep going with as many lines as your mind is willing to supply. As with your timed writing, don't stop to correct, find better words, or to rhyme. Don't focus on that now. The important thing is the idea. When you've run out of ideas, stop for a minute and read what you have written.

What story is being presented? What images or ideas does that invoke? Does that make you think of any new lines to add to your lyric? If so, write them down, too.

When You Have Nothing to Add

You've looked at your circled lines/ideas and found one that stood out as interesting, but you can't think of any new lyric lines to add to it. Never fear. This is where it pays to do another timed writing. Start by writing your selected line on a new page. Then write whatever comes to mind for the next 10 minutes. Concentrate on quick descriptions of the images and events you think of. Don't try to rhyme or structure, just write down whatever comes up.

When time is up, read what you wrote and circle anything you find interesting. Do any of the newly-circled lines add to your original? If so, go back and add them.

Still Stumped

This isn't unusual, and it says nothing about your ability to write lyrics. You may want to reread your timed writing. Are you trying to force your writing toward what you originally thought your line was about? If so, your writing might seem lifeless. Or does your mind seem to have gone completely off-topic? Think about why that may be. Is that new topic more interesting than the original one? Can you see some connection between the images or events that you hadn't been aware of before? If so, this could make a very good lyric choice. Explore it.

There are times, though, when our minds are so clouded by other things that the topic we want to work on just won't develop. When this happens, just go with it. Do a timed writing for however long you need, 10 minutes minimum. Use it to whine, complain, bemoan, or rail against everything you need to get out of your system. You never have to show this to anyone. Once again, read what you wrote. It might make you uncomfortable to read it, but you need to acknowledge it and let it go. You can destroy it if you'd like. System cleared, you'll be ready to write on your topic.

Do a new timed writing using your originally selected line, and see where it takes you this time.

One After the Other

If you're still having trouble, you can try writing one line at a time as they pop into your head, this time in lyrical/poetic structure. Write the interesting line from your list on the first line of a new page in your notebook. On the next, write a line that pops into your head. On the next, the next line that pops into your head, and so on.

This will sometimes result in utter nonsense. That's okay. You're trying to get yourself to think in lyrical format and to turn off that critic in your head that tells you it's too hard. Keep trying.

Example of a nonsense lyric:

Energetic, Ticking with life
Surrendered to the inevitable envy
 Foreign weights
Among golden gates
Locked up seven steps above

However did we get here?
Triple down and barely bought
 If heaven could afford me
I'd be checking out the south

Restless weakened
Scooped out light
Trickling into plenty
When nonsense riddles
Through this brain
Uncapes the masked inmate

Waters blown And bursting out
Spilled over sacred acres
Resting night
And weakened sheath
On quiet evening's frenzy

I still have no idea what it means, but it got me thinking in lyrical structure, and I was then able to move on. If nothing else, use this exercise to prove yourself capable on those days when you're harboring doubt.

Finishing Your Draft

So you've got a few rough lines written, maybe enough for a couple verses. Now what? This is where I start paying attention to the rhythm of the lines. Think about nursery rhymes. Notice their rhythm and the length of the lines in each verse. This structure is a good place to begin because it will be familiar and predictable. Contrasting your lyrics against those of a nursery rhyme will also give you a good sense of how your lines will fit into music.

In finishing my draft, I also look at what my verses are conveying. If they are all saying varying degrees of the same thing, I change them in order to add new information. If I don't do this, each successive verse becomes a version of blah blah blah, resulting in an automatic tune out from the audience.

For example, if each verse is describing the appearance of a woman named Julia, it's likely to be dull. Try describing Julia in one verse, then talk about her work in another and her boyfriend—or how you'd like to be her boyfriend—in another. It doesn't really matter what things you talk about, as long as they add something new. If the listener has already heard it, they won't bother listening to the rest.

If I have a rhyme scheme at this point, I evaluate whether it works. I don't get fussy about the actual rhymed words, though. These are placeholders until I find better ones. And yes, they irritate me when I look at them and think, "Geez, these are awful," but the point is to keep moving forward. This is an overview. You're focusing on structure and conveying your idea. Details later. If you focus too long in the early stages, you'll likely lose your momentum.

One More Try

So you're still having trouble coming up with a beginning lyric? No problem. Think of a song you know well, preferably something simple, with a clear melody and a lyrical structure that is easy to follow. Pop songs are a good place to start, but prog rock is usually not—though Rush's verses are pretty well defined. Choose something you think will be easy for you to mimic. Use that artist's melody, their lyrical timing, and write your own words in place of theirs. Voilà!

Keep in mind, this is only for practice. Though there are many instances in jazz and blues where lyrics have been replaced and music re-recorded, it is not commonly acceptable to do so.

If all else fails, set the lyric aside and come back to it on another day. It happens sometimes, but try to run through as many attempts as you can before setting it aside. Next day, reread your timed writing and, if nothing jumps out at you, move on to another topic.

Distraction

It's best to get in the practice of writing on a regular schedule. This may seem hard, but if you make it a habit, you'll find it easier to keep distraction at bay.

Distraction comes easily, especially with kids, pets, TV, Internet, and everything else that tries to draw your attention away from the task at hand. But sometimes the distraction is simply avoidance; it's important to know the difference. For some reason, there always seems to be something working to keeping us from what we really want to do. It usually happens with creative activities or health-related goals. If writing is something important to you and not just something you feel you should be doing, you'll know when you're simply avoiding it.

When you find yourself distracted, it's helpful to offer yourself a reward for following through on your goal. You can watch TV, read, or clean the kitchen when you're done. Until then, do what you intended to do.

Chapter 2

Inspiration & Inspired Writing

Inspiration can come from many places. Your ideas, thoughts, observations, and dreams can be the source of your inspiration. They put you onto a topic. They're the beginning. That's why you've been writing those lines in the back of your notebook.

Inspired writing, on the other hand, sounds pretty mystical. I really can't explain where it comes from. Entire verses, choruses, poems, or blog postings pop into your head as you scramble to get it all down. At times like this, it doesn't seem like you're driving the pen or your fingers. When this happens, you can choose to believe what you'd like about the source. Whatever makes you comfortable with accepting the ideas being given—whether from yourself, your muse, the divine—is right. There are no wrong answers here.

When I started out writing rudimentary poems and was thinking about writing lyrics, I sometimes experienced inspired writing. I started to believe I was supposed to wait for inspiration. So I waited. And waited. And waited. But I didn't get any more inspiration until I started putting in my time. I believe those early, inspired writings were prompts to keep me going. When I stopped doing any work on my own, I got no more freebies.

Some people wait for inspiration before they begin, but they often wait a long time. They get frustrated, and when it does finally hit them, it's often not of the quality you might expect. I believe inspired writing comes as a gift for putting in the daily work, and from my experience, the quality of the writing improves with your own improvement. You get back what you put in.

Note: Some writers believe they should never change a word when it comes to this type of inspired writing. I don't believe that's the intention. Get it down, but feel free to change what doesn't fit your personality or vocabulary. If you believe the inspiration is coming from outside of you, or even if you believe it is from an unconscious part within you, think of it as collaboration. The chosen words aren't fixed. The idea behind the words—the sentiment, lesson, or story—is far more important than keeping all the words exactly as they're dictated. It's my belief that if the idea seems like something worth sharing, it's better to edit it to your taste than to shelve it.

Chapter 3

Perfect Rhyme's Not Always So Perfect

When the vowel and consonants of two words share the same sound, this is called a perfect rhyme. Examples would be right rhymed with kite or flow rhymed with glow. It's all about sound, not spelling.

When used deliberately to draw attention or to get people to sing along, perfect rhyme can be a great tool. If used only to fit a perfect rhyme scheme, however, it can be tiresome, or worse, cliché. There are only so many perfect rhymes available for any given word. Sometimes this makes it difficult to find a perfectly rhymed word that best suits the lyric. It'll have you rhyming ink with sink or love with glove, simply because you're short on options.

Beginning lyric writers tend to rely heavily on perfect rhyme. It's recognizable. The words are easy to think of, and it looks like what you're supposed to do. But it's limiting. It can take a great idea and make it bland or make a compelling story sound trite.

Get acquainted with imperfect rhyming, also called near-rhyme. It'll open up a whole world of possibilities, and it sounds darn close. An example would be wool rhymed with all or town rhymed with ground. They're close but not exact.

A rhyming dictionary is a great investment and one that can help you find the right rhyming word without distorting your meaning. It allows you to look up possible rhymes by sound. Many of them even discuss types of rhyme, stressed syllables, and poetic devices. All great stuff to add to your lyric writing tool belt.

If you listen to a lot of Top 40 songs from the 70s or even current pop music, you'll hear a lot of perfect rhymes. Some are done well, some not so much. Let your ears be your guide.

Which ones made you think? Maybe you were expecting a different word or expecting the word to be in a different spot in the rhyming line. These deliberate uses of perfect rhyme are meant to draw your attention.

In which songs does the use of perfect rhyme make you cringe or roll your eyes every time you hear them? Could you accurately predict the rhyming word they chose, or did it seem like they plunked that word in just to make it rhyme? Make note, and try to keep the things you dislike out of your own lyrics.

Rhyming can be tricky, because you want to choose words that stay true to your lyric's meaning. Perfect rhyming tends to make the beginning writer stray from their original meaning simply to make the rhyme fit. This takes away from the lyric. There are always exceptions, though, and as you learn, you'll begin to notice when it's used well and when it's not.

Note: Rhymed words don't always have to land at the end of line 2 and 4, nor do they even have to land at the end of any line. We'll have a look at this later on.

When to Rhyme

Some people love rules. I'm not one of them. As a new dabbler in the art of lyric writing, you shouldn't be, either. That's not to say that you should avoid rhyming altogether. It's a staple in the old bag of tricks, and you should learn to use it well enough to know when you can get away without it.

How to Use Rhyme

When beginning, it is normal to start by rhyming the end words of lines 2 and 4 in a 4- line verse. It's fairly standard. In nursery rhymes, you'll find this is usually where the rhymed words are placed. This is why it's a good reference model. Let's get to work.

Start on a new page in your notebook. Copy the main parts of each line, leaving the end- rhyme spots on lines 2 and 4 blank. If using a computer, make a copy of your original file. You'll make changes to the copy. The original will be used as a reference later on.

If you've already placed rhyming words in your lyrics, you can skip this next part.

Start out by using perfect rhyme in the placeholder spots—the end words—on line 2 and line 4. Once you've placed rhyming words in all your verses, read through the entire lyric.

You may cringe at your word choices, but don't let that get in the way. You'll make adjustments later on.

Note: I'm concentrating on 4-line verses here, since they are the most common. The length, of course, isn't a rule. Your verse length will depend on several factors. We'll take a look at this in Chapter 8, Advanced Techniques.

Using a Thesaurus to Improve Rhyme Choices

Your perfect rhymes are in their places, and you're itching to get better words onto paper, aren't you? Good. This is the time to look back at your original lyric. Do your rhyming words convey your intended idea, or do they dull or skew it?

Let's look at the first verse. Do either of your rhyming words convey the right idea? If not, get out a thesaurus. If you don't have a thesaurus, it would be a good idea to buy one. Many computers have a thesaurus built into their word processing applications, and there are also many available on the Internet. Any of these are good if you don't have a copy available, but a copy of Roget's Thesaurus is always a good investment, as synonyms are laid out by meaning, rather than alphabetically. This means you can find other words related to the subject of your lyric, as well as synonyms for words you have already placed. This may lead you to ideas, themes, or words you hadn't already considered.

Using your thesaurus, look up each of the words you originally wrote on lines 2 and 4, whether they rhyme or not. Examine the list of possible synonyms. On a new page in your notebook, make a list of the ones that appeal to you. It's best to choose words you would be likely to use yourself.

Select the word from your list that appeals most but stays true to your meaning. If you're having trouble selecting one, go with your instinct at this point. You want to keep moving forward.

Now look at the list of synonyms you came up with for your second word. Do any of these words rhyme with your newly selected first rhyming word? If not, do any of them seem like the right word for this line? This is where you may get in a bit of a tug-of-war between your newly selected words. Don't worry about it too much for now. Make note of your preferred words, and get out your rhyming dictionary.

Let's take a look at the first rhymed word again. Look up that word in your rhyming dictionary. Take a look at the suggestions provided, make note of the ones that interest you, then look them up. This part may take a little while, but is well worth it.

With practice, you will find that the other verses' rhymes come together more easily. If they don't right now, that's okay. You're making the effort. Eventually, you'll start thinking in rhyme. Just keep at it.

About Choruses

If you're rhyming lines 2 and 4 in your verses, experiment with rhyming different lines in the chorus. It gives the listener's ears a surprise. Wake 'em up. Try rhyming line 1 with line 3, line 3 with line 4, or line 1 with line 4.

Choruses are a bit of a different animal. Sometimes they can be as simple as one line repeated—John Mayer often uses this method in his pop songs. Or it could be two lines. Some songs use vocalizations as the chorus, and some use a standard 4-line—or more—method. Your selection should be based on what works best to sum up or accentuate the verses in your lyric.

Sometimes, choruses emerge during the meshing of the lyrics to music, so don't be so set in your idea that you don't recognize what might work better.

Experiment. Be adventurous. Pay attention to the choruses in songs you enjoy, and practice writing similar ones. It's all experience.

Chapter 4

I've Got Rhythm

Rhythm is very important to lyric lines. It creates movement—or deliberately stops it. The types of words you choose, the length of your lines, and the way the words are vocalized all contribute to rhythm. Because of this, you need to learn about stressed and unstressed syllables. It's not as difficult as it sounds. It's about how we speak words —which syllable gets the biggest emphasis. This would be the stressed syllable.

For example, the word balance is stressed on the first syllable: Ba-lance. The second syllable is softer, not as attention-grabbing and, therefore, not stressed.

You'll find that many songs have 4 stressed syllables for line 1 and line 3, and 3 stressed syllables for lines 2 and 4, but this isn't always true. Listen to your favorite songs, and see if you can determine how many stressed syllables each line holds.

Right now you're probably thinking, "But I've already written my lyric and changed the rhymes. I have to do more?" Yes. Anyone can write a lyric, as you did in chapter one, but to write a good lyric, you need to keep working at it.

Shining a Light

Have a look again at the first verse you wrote. Read each line through, and if you feel comfortable enough, read it out loud. If you wrote your lyric using a familiar song as the framework, you probably have a pretty set rhythm already in place. That is to say, you likely mimicked their stressed syllables as well as their line lengths.

In nursery rhymes such as Mary Had a Little Lamb, lines 2 and 4 end on a stressed word. Stressed words stand out. When they also rhyme, they draw a lot of attention. When sung, it will become the focus and may be the only word that some listeners remember in that line. So it's pretty darn important.

Look again at your rhymed words. It is likely that they are also stressed. But if not, you may want to revise the lines.

This is where poetry and lyrics become divergent. In poetry, it is acceptable to end a line on an odd word. Phrases may seem disjointed. The ending of a line is intended to indicate a pause. But in music, this doesn't tend to come across clearly. It may sound strange.

In song, two lines will often combine to complete a sentence. Each of those lines is usually sung within its own bar of music, but this isn't always true. Dependent on music, each line could potentially be sung over more than one bar. In those cases, each line should feel somewhat stable on its own, though you may not become aware of it until you are crafting a melody. Just something to keep in mind when looking at the entire verse.

As you get more practice and figure out what works, you'll be able to determine when you can get away with a different line structure. For now, I would suggest you stick to the basic structure I've outlined: the 4/3/4/3 stressed syllables.

Back to your rhymed words. Do they draw too much, too little, or just the right amount of attention? Which words stand out the most in your lyric? Think about how you would speak these lines.

Thinking of your line as though it were dialogue can help. If the line you've written would sound odd as a line of conversation, you may want to revise it. We tend to put natural pauses and stresses into the way we speak. Think about where you would breathe when speaking the lines.

Could those be natural breaks for your lyric? If so, do they end on a stressed word?

Here's what I mean about a line feeling odd. If your lyric is based in present day and intended for a modern audience, but it sounds like Victorian poetry, your lyric probably won't work. It will sound odd or dated. Write your lines as you would speak them or write them on a to-do list.

Example of a list or note sort of lyric:

Dashing out to get some milk

Will be home by ten

If I'm late, please don't forget

To bring the paper in.

I would suggest, for your own reference, to count the number of stressed syllables in each of your lines. If they aren't balanced in the 4/3/4/3 method, try rewriting to make them so.

Reread the verse and see if it feels better. If not, you can change it back.

Most people tend to choose strong words for the rhyming spots out of instinct—it probably goes back to the nursery rhymes—but if you didn't, this is your opportunity to rewrite those lines. Though sometimes all it takes is a little shuffling, as you'll see in the next chapter.

Chapter 5

Making it Better

Your lyric is written—with or without a chorus—your rhymes chosen, and it seems okay . . . but not great. Don't worry, there's a lot you can do to spiff 'em up. You can shuffle the lines around, swap words, slide your rhyming word to another spot, and you can clean up any unnecessary words.

Clean House

If you remove all the extraneous words, does the lyric still make sense? For example, if your first line is 'The black cat lay on a tin roof,' and you change it to 'Black cat on a tin roof,' do you still have the same intended meaning? It's easy to get in the habit of forming complete sentences, but in lyrical or poetic form, this isn't necessary. Play around with it. Change until to 'til or around to 'round. Evict the unnecessary words or syllables, and see if it improves your lyric.

The Old Switcheroo

A complete rewrite of a line isn't always needed. Sometimes you can get away with rearranging the words in the line or the lines within a verse. Have a look at any of the lines that are bothering you, and see if you might arrange the words in some other way that still makes sense. If that doesn't seem possible, what if you were to rearrange your lines? This would, of course, shift your rhyming positions, but could make your verse more interesting. Try it and see if there is any improvement.

Nothing wrong with swapping verses around either. This won't work for story lyrics, where you intend to move from one event to the next, but it can make other lyrics stronger or simply give you another perspective.

Remember, we're just practicing here, so don't get too attached to anything just yet.

Into the Thick of It

You're still not done. Now that you're familiar with rhythm, rhyming, stressed and unstressed syllables, and how those draw attention, it's time to look at what your lines are saying. Does each new line add a little bit more information or interest? It should. Take a look at the following:

I'm so darn sad

Feelin' oh so down

I'm so depressed

Just like I'm drowning

Yes, there are 4 lines that follow the 4/3/4/3 stressed syllable pattern, but other than the first line, I really haven't said anything. At this point, the listener is thinking, "This person is sad. Got it." Then they stop listening. If you've got a really great chorus, they might tune back in, but odds are you've lost them.

So what do you do? Start asking questions. In this case: Why is this person sad? Did he just get dumped? Did her pet die? What event might have triggered this sadness? Did the person cause this event themselves or was it something external—like losing a job?

Other questions you might consider asking yourself to improve your lyrical choices:

Where is this happening? Don't just name it; describe it as vividly as possible—sights, sounds, smells.

Who are the characters in your story?

Why did this event happen? Why did the story need telling?

What is happening or has happened?

How did this situation occur?

When did it take place? Don't just name it. Describe how the sunrise looked over the mountaintop before the mining company came to call.

So, to review, ask the where, what, when, why, who, and how questions that relate to your story. Do timed writing for each to flush out ideas, then slot in your new details.

Clarifying Point of View

It's easy to get distracted by the individual lines, but now it's time to look at your lyric as a whole and ensure that your points of view and verb tenses are in agreement. This means that if the perspective is first person, you should make sure that either all verses are written from that perspective or that changing to another point of view makes sense. You don't want to refer to yourself in the third person in one verse and first person in the rest.

Verb agreement is important, too. If Johnny is going somewhere in the first verse, it's okay for him to arrive, but it shouldn't suddenly become past tense. There are some very specific times when this sort of thing may work; for instance, if Johnny is recounting a memory as though he were back in that time. That is a very tricky place to go, though. I'd suggest keeping it simple.

Recount your memories in the past tense, but if you want the action happening now, keep it in the present.

This is another opportunity to play with your lyric. You've written it from one perspective, but how would it look if you changed it to another? If your lyric is written in the third person perspective—he/she—could it be stronger if changed to first person? Try it and see. Get a look at it from a different point of view. Sometimes distance can be used to make a somewhat personal lyric more accessible to the listener. This can be used for a subject that is a bit uncomfortable. It can allow both you and your listeners to be observers. Taking a third person account and making it first person makes it more intimate, inviting the listener in. Play around with it. You'll know when it feels like you've got the right perspective.

Chapter 6

More Tools

You already have a few ways to improve your lyrics. Here are a few more that are worth learning.

Metaphors & Similes

Metaphors and similes are powerful tools. They may seem intimidating at first, but it's not that hard to create your own. Your timed writings can be a great place to begin.

Similes use the words like or as to compare one thing to another. Metaphors actually declare one thing to be another. Metaphors paint a vivid picture in the listener's mind.

Example of a simile: He's as tall as a building.

Example of a metaphor: He had mountains of laundry still to be done.

In your timed writing, you probably used similes when describing how something looked, smelled, felt, tasted, or sounded. This is good. Use these. Similes can be scattered throughout or used sparingly to help clarify a line. Similes are demonstrative.

So if you write 'my house is as big as a mountain,' you're giving the listener a good idea that you have a pretty large house. If, on the other hand, you write 'my house is a mountain,' you're going to have your listener picturing a cave opening. Nothing wrong with that, so long as that is your intention.

Try turning some of the similes you find in your timed writing into metaphors. If you find you like some of the metaphors you create, write them in the back of your notebook with your interesting lines.

Contradiction & Sarcasm

Contradiction is similar to sarcasm, but often with less of the biting tone. What comes to mind is Sting's song I'm So Happy I Can't Stop Crying. The title is already contradicting itself—as do the lyrics—and the music has an upbeat feel. Sting has mentioned in interviews that this song is about divorce. This is a fine example of what I mean.

The best use of sarcasm I've heard has been in country songs. Few others are able to pull it off. That may be because of the way country music is sung. With that twang, the message seems to come across loud and clear. If you use sarcasm, you might need to experiment with how you vocalize the words.

Write Extra Verses

In a Wikipedia article, it's mentioned that Leonard Cohen may have written as many as 80 verses for his song Hallelujah. That's dedication! He clearly felt strongly enough about that song to continue working on it long past the point where others would have given up. I'm not suggesting that you write 80 different verses for your lyric, but it's always good to write a few extras. You may find them better than those you already had, or they may demonstrate an aspect of your idea that you hadn't yet explored.

Mash 'em up

With your extra verses, read over the entirety of what you wrote. Try switching your verses around with the earlier ones, exchanging words, or swapping some of the lines from your extra verses into your earlier ones. In my experience, it has often resulted in much clearer verses and, usually, a much stronger lyric.

Chapter 7

Working with Other Musicians to Develop a Melody

Melody is what can take a poem and turn it into a lyric. Crafting an interesting melody can make a big difference in how your lyric is perceived. If you're writing the music, melody, and lyrics, you have a lot of control. But working with other musicians can often be helpful in coming up with melodies you may not have thought of on your own.

A note about the musicians you work with: Find musicians that will allow you to try a few different melodies before giving up. If at all possible—and I know this is a difficult task—find people who are interested in exploring music rather than expecting perfection at the first crack.

Find people who are willing to work with you, rather than against you. Until that time, though, work on your own melodies. Record them and listen back. Keep working at it.

Another note: It would be helpful, in the long run, to acquire at least a rudimentary knowledge of music, either by learning to play an instrument, ear training, or learning music theory.

Timing is vital to melody. If you're having trouble understanding where to come in or how to judge when a bar is starting or ending, it would be a good idea to work with a metronome. If you don't play an instrument, playing percussion instruments to the sound of a metronome is also a good way to learn about timing. Another is to determine the proper tempos for some of your favorite songs. Set your metronome to the appropriate tempo and practice the lyrics a cappella. You may think you know the song well, but without accompaniment, you'll find it more difficult. With the metronome as your guide, you'll learn to feel the rhythm.

Most of the melodies I have created came about while working with a band. As we're piecing together music, I determine which of my lyrics might fit and run through them in my head, paying attention to the length of the lines and how I might sing them. Then I try out a melody. This is generally instinctual. This is why knowing how to play an instrument or having ear training will be extremely helpful.

That being said, some of the melodies I've come up with were created on my own, without the use of an instrument or a band. I recorded them a cappella on a digital recorder and stored the files on my computer. When I'm looking for ideas, I go back and listen to those recordings. I rarely think of them while I'm working with the band, but the melodies sometimes make their way into songs—though I often don't recall that I'd previously recorded them. It's only when I listen to them again or hear someone humming the melody that it dawns on me. That alone should give you reason to experiment with melody on your own time.

If you're having trouble finding patient musicians, and you're not yet comfortable with creating your own melodies, I suggest you listen to music you enjoy. Pay attention to how their melodies mesh with the music. Do they follow closely? Do they stick to simple melodies, or are they more complicated? Are the notes mirroring those of the guitar/piano, or are they complementary?

Stick to simple melodies at first—think of those nursery rhymes again. With experience, you'll be able to make your melodies more complex.

As a side note, have a listen to Stevie Ray Vaughn's take on Mary Had a Little Lamb. I think you'll find it kind of cool that his rhythm doesn't stray too far from the original nursery rhyme. It might even give you some ideas about turning those nursery-rhyme-based lyrics you've been writing into actual song lyrics.

Chapter 8

Advanced

Techniques

Verse Length

Although many songs are written using a 4-line verse, you can write verses in any length you wish. Your music and melody will help you determine when you should vary the length of your lines or revise what you've already written. As you gain experience, you'll find your judgment about verse length will also improve.

If your 6-line verse fits nicely into 4 bars of music, you can think of it in the same way you would a standard 4-line verse. However, if you're having difficulty fitting your lyric into 4 bars, your lyric may need to be broken up into more lines, or it may need to be revised. The length of your lines can be a clue. At this point, I will assume that you've already removed extraneous words.

Think, once again, about how you would say these lines and also how you'll sing them. Where do you pause? Where do you take breaths? Could this be a natural break for the line? Take time, also, to consider whether you could drop a line or add a new one.

Very long lines in your verse will be more difficult to squeeze in or may require 2 bars of music each. It doesn't need to be complicated. Do your best to fit your lyric into the music, and work with the other musicians to fit in your lines as needed.

Line Length

There are a number of reasons to vary line length. One is to set a feel or a mood for the verse. An abrupt ending to the verse, by shortening the last line, will make the verse feel off kilter. The listener is expecting the usual 4/3/4/3 stressed pattern, and when they don't hear it, it feels unbalanced. If you want a balanced feel, count the stressed syllables in each line and alter them accordingly.

Try experimenting with varying line lengths. Notice how the balance is tipped when you do so. Does this help your lyric, or does it contradict the emotion you're trying to convey?

Depending on how they're sung, lines that include lots of short words can mimic a hurried feel. Think of Led Zeppelin's Immigrant Song. It feels like they're rushing. If they'd used fewer words, it wouldn't have the same feel and may not have worked. Conversely, lines with longer words, more vowels that are sung at a slower pace, or vowel sounds that are drawn out will feel more relaxed.

Experiment with all of these, and keep them in your tool bag. You never know when one of them could rescue an otherwise dull lyric.

Alternate Rhyme Schemes

End rhymes land at the end of a line in your verse. Note that this is not always on lines 2 and 4. I started with rhyming line 2 with line 4, because this is fairly common in nursery rhymes, but you can rhyme any of your lines—or all of them. In Sheryl Crow's My Favorite Mistake, she rhymed the first 2 lines of her verse. The Police rhyme every line in Every Breath You Take. The perceived 5th line in that song—which doesn't rhyme—is actually a refrain or pre-chorus.

End rhymes are just one method, though. You can also rhyme words within your line, either in addition to, or excluding the end rhyme. This can be a surprise for the listeners. We've been conditioned to expect them at the end of the line, so hearing a rhyme somewhere else can make a listener's ears perk up. But don't do it just for shock value; if it doesn't make sense to do so, then don't! As always, make sure it works for your lyric.

You can also—gasp!—choose not to rhyme at all. Despite what some people believe, it is completely acceptable. This method is just another available tool. When you hear music, rhyme is somewhat expected, but isn't actually necessary. Sometimes the rhythm is enough. You need to be the judge. Don't let this be an excuse to be lazy about selecting the right words, though. You'll know when it feels right.

Improve Your Melody

Sometimes when creating melody we tend to focus solely on melody and forget the words we're singing. Because of this, we might put emphasis on words that shouldn't get the attention. Suddenly, the normally unstressed word or syllable is in the spotlight. To fix this, read your lyrics and speak each line as though you were saying it in conversation. Where would the emphasis normally be placed?

I have noticed that when singing my lyrics for the first time, I tend to put emphasis on the wrong syllable—the a in above, for instance. When I do this, I don't always notice right away, but it sounds strange. Think about how you'd actually say the word. If you're stressing a normally unstressed syllable, change it so that you're stressing the appropriate part of the word. This usually sounds better, but, again, you must be the judge.

Kill Your Darlings

The title of this section, a partial quote from William Faulkner in regards to writing, is also appropriate for lyric writing. It's easy to get attached to the words we've labored over, but it can sometimes be in your best interest to let them go.

When working on melody, it can be tempting to cling to every last syllable you've worked hard to craft, but this can be a mistake. If the music is great and your melody is coming along, but the words seem too hurried, wordy, or sparse, you may need to revise your lyrics again.

If hurried or wordy, perhaps you can pare down those lyric lines even further. If too sparse, perhaps you could make 2 verses into one or rewrite to fit the new music. You have to be willing to let them go, if that's what it takes to create a better-fitting lyric.

From a psychological perspective, when I finish a lyric —whether I've created a melody or not—I read through it, let myself feel a bit proud, then let it go. I've said what needed to be said, expressed what felt right, and crafted it to the best of my ability. I think of them as being in the wind and give myself permission to lose my attachment to them. This is all very Zen, I know, but if you can let go of your attachment, you'll find it easier to do the necessary revisions. Put the words aside and move on.

Chapter 9

Check Your

Attitude

No matter who you meet, there is always something you can learn from them. Though our society often promotes competition, I see it as unhealthy when it comes to validating your work or the work of others. It's art. Some will like it, some won't. When we compare, especially in a negative way, what we are saying is that we feel insecure.

Not liking something is far different from saying something sucks. It's perfectly legitimate to say you don't get it, or you don't like it, but to say something sucks can never be taken as any sort of valid opinion. It's not cool, and it says more about your feelings than their ability. Your art is not in competition with theirs, so there is no need to justify it. Keep doing your thing. Keep improving.

Keeping this in mind, don't be too quick to show all your new lyrics to just anyone. Lyrics are often personal. Some people won't get them. Some people will insist they don't like poetry, but will sing along when the song comes out. Some people will evaluate your grammar and spelling, just to take the wind out of your sails. And some will be like the guy I mentioned above and say your lyrics suck. If you feel the need to share, find a person—or people, if you're lucky—who will be kind. You probably have an idea of who the likely candidates are.

When you've been doing this a while and you've gained some confidence, you won't care so much what people think.

Chapter 10

Putting it all Together

I've walked you through the various stages I take to write lyrics. Let's recap.

Generate ideas by doing timed writings of at least 10 minutes, exploring all your senses.

Be careful of waiting for inspiration.

Place your rhymes; revise your rhymes. Work on the rhythm of your lines.

Revise your lyric for clarity and improvement.

Have a look at other tools you can employ to improve your lyrics even more.

Work with other musicians to create melodies.

Try out some more advanced tools.

I hope this book has helped demystify some of the methods for lyric writing, and that you now feel confident that you, too, can write lyrics. You've taken the first steps, and if you keep at it, and keep learning, you'll just keep getting better.

Best of luck, and have fun!

One more thing

You'll come across people who tell you that there is a right way and a wrong way to write lyrics. There isn't. There are guidelines and methods, but that's it. It's called art for a reason. Listen to their advice, try out their methods, but if they ultimately don't work, feel free to discard them. In fact, you should try all sorts of methods—anything you can think of or any suggestions you read about.

Don't take it personally if someone says you're doing it wrong. It's just that they've found what works for them, or they've bought into the myth that there is only one way to write lyrics. Believing this, though, is limiting and will quickly become an obstacle. Don't fall into that trap.

With lyric writing, you'll find that what works one day may not work the next, so it's helpful to have a number of different methods you can try. Eventually, you'll find the ones that produce your best results. Be flexible and open to new methods, and you'll continue to fill your lyric writing trick bag. Remember that it's art, and art is constantly being transformed. Be adventurous. You'll know when you've hit on the methods that work for you.

Appendix Further Reading

There are a number of books that have helped me immensely, and I'm sure will help you, too. Here is a very brief list:

Lyric Writing

Writing Down the Bones - Natalie Goldberg

Write Better Lyrics - Pat Pattison

Poetry for Dummies - John Timpane, Maureen Watts

Reference Books

The Complete Rhyming Dictionary - edited by Clement Wood, revised by Ronald Bogus

Roget's Thesaurus

Other Reading

Poetry - Although the thought of reading poetry may bore you, there is much to learn from it about rhythm and rhyme. You may very well find new things to try by reading what others have done.

Lyrics - Some artists post their lyrics on their websites; others have published books. You can often find lyrics posted on lyric websites. These are unauthorized and are often submitted by fans. Keep in mind that they may not be correct.

Songwriters on Songwriting - Paul Zollo

I found it fascinating to read about the methodologies of various artists. I learned that right and wrong, in regards to writing and composing, are nonexistent. It gave me permission to find what worked for me.

The War of Art, Turning Pro - Steven Pressfield

Both are excellent books exploring how artists work and what keeps us from doing the work we most want to do.

Acknowledgements

I would like to thank my editor, Susan Hughes @ http://myindependenteditor.com, Brenda Carol for helping me expand my idea of what is possible as a a singer (even if it took me a bit longer than expected), and my husband, Chris for being my first reader and encouraging me when I needed it.

About the Author

Shel Craig is a singer, writer and lyricist who resides in Southern Ontario with her drummer husband and two cats.